The Confident Rider Mindset
(How to hack your mind for riding success)

Dr Tracey Cole

© Copyright Tracey Cole

All rights reserved.

No part of this book may be reproduced by any mechanical, electronic or photographic process, or in the form of a phonographic recording; nor may it be stored in a retrieval system, transmitted or otherwise be copied, other than for 'fair use' as brief quotations embodied in articles, without the prior permission of the author.

The information given in this book should not be treated as a substitute for professional advice. Any use of this book is at the reader's discretion and risk. The author cannot be held responsible for any loss, claim or damage arising out of the use, or misuse, of the suggestions made, the failure to seek professional advice or for any material on third-party websites.

ISBN: 9781797636542

Design & typesetting by Socciones Editoria Digitale
www.socciones.co.uk

To Mum, Dad, Martin & all the horses I've had the pleasure to ride and own

Contents

Welcome!...1

1. Loosening up our way of thinking..3

2. A tour of the conscious and unconscious minds..12

3. Beliefs..20

4. Removing limiting beliefs...26

5. Breaking down the problem even more!...35

6. Diminishing and dissolving fears...38

7. More advanced mind techniques...46

8. What to do whilst riding - building confidence whilst in the saddle.............................51

9. FAQs and closing comments..57

About the author..60

Welcome!

As a former nervous rider, particularly when it came to hacking, mounting, competing, jumping (actually, almost everything!), I was amazed that I overcame my fears. That was something that happened to other people. I thought my mind was too stubborn and my nerves too ingrained to ever really enjoy all aspects of riding. I thought that I should know my limits and that it was other people went out and about enjoying their rides. I always had a huge feeling of relief when I got off my horse and I mistook that for enjoyment!! Whilst I was actually on the horse, well, I was sometimes frozen like a statue wondering why I put myself through it! However, using a combination of techniques, I was very, very surprised (and delighted) that I overcame my fears – to the extent that I couldn't get them back! When I enrolled on an NLP (neurolinguistic programming) training, it was such a massive surprise that I got rid of my fears, that I tested myself over and over and tried to get them back. But I couldn't! (I really do not advise that you try to get fears back, it was something that I had to test before I made this my job!)

The only way to be entirely confident in anything at all, is to engage the unconscious (i.e. subconscious) mind. That's it! If you already do something confidently e.g., driving, cooking or something to do with your work, your unconscious mind is engaged and on board. The unconscious stores all our memories, habits and emotions, it's exactly the part of the mind we need to work with to change the way we think and act.

Conversely, if you've ever tried to use reasoning and logic to overcome riding nerves, you're engaging the conscious mind. Talking yourself confident, or having someone else try to convince you of your riding capabilities, rarely works. The unconscious mind, running the show behind the scenes, has not been consulted.

Writing this book has been a true labour of love and I'm so excited about it! I've gone back to the time when I was a static passenger hoping for a ride without incident and without feeling a complete idiot. I've researched what works and what works fast and efficiently. How to style a multi-pronged attack on the mind, to get those fears pummelled into the dust.

We start by opening up the mind to change, persuading the mind that there is another way to ride. Then we get into changing the mind. These easy and effective techniques are not theory-based. Everything is highly practical, do-able and fun. There are plenty of quick techniques to try out, as well as tasks to keep you thinking, consciously and unconsciously about your riding confidence goals. Some of the methods are perfect to do whilst in the saddle too.

I've purposefully devised each chapter to provide your unconscious mind with a comprehensive range of techniques and cumulative ideas to change your thinking. This means making new pathways and connections between the nerve cells in your mind; this book changes your neurology! However, it works optimally when each chapter is completed in order. It's not a book to dip into and flick from page to page. I'd say for the best results, the exercises shouldn't be skipped or rushed, they are there to pave the way to confidence by opening the minds to new thoughts and then new behaviours. If a job's worth doing, it's worth doing well, so let's not create a flimsy, superficial riding confidence, but a robust one, built on solid foundations. To some people, foundation building may not seem worth the effort, but it' this section of the book that will enable your mind to change more easily and more effortlessly when we start the change work; it is the difference between getting it done and getting it done well. We'll get back to the basics of how the unconscious mind works, clear away our current mindset, strip away old, limiting ideas and build up again, layer by layer. The only exception to this is Chapter 8. This gives you some quick, easy techniques to do whilst riding, these can be started whenever you want and can be done in combination with the other chapters.

Using a notebook or journal to jot down your mind work and dating the changes you see and feel can be a hugely positive step for your mind to acknowledge progress and be convinced how far you've come. Take your time, this is a marathon, not a sprint, but so worth crossing the finishing line for. Remember to be of good heart and good humour, laughter and learning go hand in hand in my book.

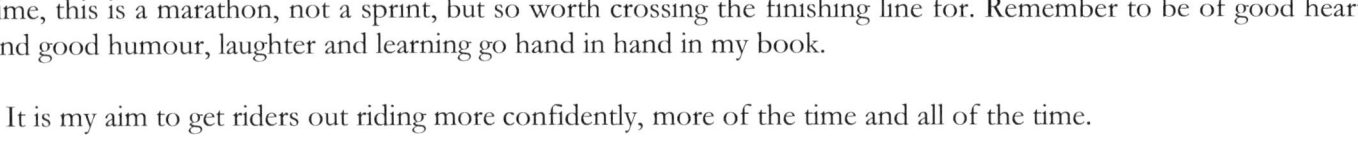

It is my aim to get riders out riding more confidently, more of the time and all of the time.

To your success!

Warmest

Tracey

Tracey Cole BSc, PhD, MABNLP, MABNLP (Coaching Division), MABH, MTLTA
Accredited Trainer and Master Coach of NLP, NLP Coaching, Hypnosis and Time Line Therapy®

1. Loosening up our way of thinking

Some riding issues are stubborn and deep-seated; others are actually so deep in the unconscious mind that we haven't uncovered them yet. If we take the time to loosen our thinking, by the time we learn how to eliminate our issues, they will be already withering away.

How are perceptions generated?

We build up a mental representation of what's happening in our personal world using our senses. As riders, this is important to be aware of, because we also build up a perception of our own ability. This is often inaccurate! In most cases, riders who are seeking to be more confident underestimate their ability and see themselves as having far less skill than they actually have. Think for a moment about the rider who wants to jump a 3 feet show-jumping course, but has a mental block on jumping higher than 2 feet 9 inches. When their horse is videoed jumping 2 feet 9 inches, it becomes apparent that they are clearing well over 2'9" and actually jumping at least 3'3". Consider the rider who dreads their horse bolting; yet whenever the horse has decided to bolt, very often one of two things occurs: the rider stops the horse or the rider is able to stay on until the horse is back in control. In the moment where they have experienced their worst-case scenario, the rider has coped admirably. The fear comes after the event, it's a second-hand response.

Knowing that we all have only a fickle grasp of reality can help to loosen our fears. Let's examine how our perceptions may not be as fixed as we think.

Our mind captures information from the external world using our 5 senses – sights, sounds, feelings, tastes and smells. If we contemplate how much information is just for the sights, we take in all the shades of every colour we see, all the nuances of brightness, contrast, shadows, depth perception, focus, whether the focus is changing or steady, of every single object. At the same time, the mind is flooded with information from all other senses too, as well as our internal self-talk making endless commentaries. This is sensory overload! As shown in the diagram of the NLP Communication Model below, every second our mind is bombarded with 2-400 billion pieces of information! So much of the information is unnecessary! The unconscious mind begins to filter out what it considers as superfluous. It's now that we can begin to understand how the filters in our mind may have imperfections that cloud or colour our thinking.

The NLP Communication Model

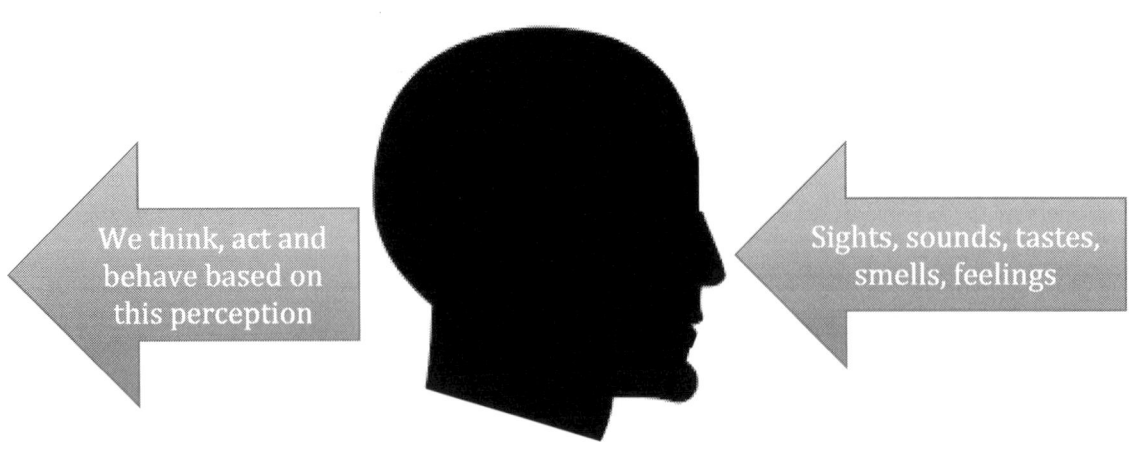

5-9 chunks of information that we're aware of ← We filter the information down to 100-2000 pieces of information ← 2-400 billion pieces of information per second

We have 3 major processing filters in the mind that cut down all that information – they are known as distortion, deletion and generalisation.

- Distortion – we amplify or diminish based on personal prejudices (e.g., making us feel that as riders we are less than equipped to be confident or making our mistakes loom large)
- Deletion – we tune out of experiences and omit them. (Have you ever had someone else recount a time when you rode really well, a time you had virtually forgotten? What about all the times you had that connection with a horse, did you forget those moments too?)
- Generalisation – making sweeping statements and drawing big conclusions, based on what may only be one or two prior experiences. (How many great or good rides have you had? How many not so good? Do you generalise more towards the not-so-good experiences? If you've changed your horse, did you continue to think about the old experiences with the old horse and expect your new horse to be the same?).

After filtering, we're still left with 100-2000 pieces of information per second, inconceivably large amounts of data for us to assimilate. Our mind then groups them for us, into a more manageable 5-9 piece chunks. This is what we deal with every second, if we're alert! So much information is simply removed from our awareness, we started with billions of pieces and been left with a handful; how can we ever have a true impression of reality?! No wonder we all have different perceptions! (And by the way, your horse's mind does this too!)

We use various key words and phrases to show where we've distorted, deleted and generalised our perceptions.

Distortions

- Listen for the times that you say that one thing means another, but the conclusion doesn't 'add up'. E.g., I'm a really experienced rider and I've ridden some flightly, spooky horses, but I'm scared to ride my current quiet horse.
- Listen for times when you think you know what others are thinking, e.g., those people who were watching me ride today, they thought I was over-horsed

How to reduce distortions, ask:

- How do you know that?
- Can you read minds?
- How can doing X cause Y?

Deletions

- Listen for where you miss out parts of the evidence and focus on a narrow version of reality. E.g. I'm a failure. Says who? At what specifically? Riding. All riding? No. Then what specifically? Cantering. Have you ever cantered well for just a few strides even?
- Non-specific use of words like 'they' or a group of people you have put together E.g.
    - They say a good rider rides with their mind. Who is 'they'?
    - Professional riders don't do that. Which professional riders, specifically? Who says that? How do you know that, specifically?

How to reduce deletions, ask:

- Who, what, how, when *specifically?*
- Ask, is that all the time? Every single time? Has that always been so?

Generalisations

You hear yourself using these words:

- Always, never, nobody, everybody
- Must, mustn't, should, shouldn't, need
- Can't, impossible, unable

How to reduce generalisations, ask:

- What can you do? Do you know anyone who does?
- What stops you?
- What if you could?
- What do you need to do? Who says?
- Nobody? Is there one person who doesn't? What tells you that?
- Always? Every time? Never? What can you do differently?

☐ **Task:** Consider in your riding where you may distort, delete and generalise your perceptions. E.g., do you remember the more unpleasant situations more than the enjoyable ones? Do you tend to delete information about your talents around horses? Do you think others are judging you? Do you generalise by expecting each ride to be challenging? Keep a journal or notebook of your distortions, deletions and generalisations.

When recovering the detail from filtered thoughts and impressions, it's important **not** to ask yourself, "Why?" e.g., "Why do I always do X?". If you were to say, "Why do I always find it difficult to remain calm?" The word 'why' assumes that it's difficult, it reinforces the assumption that there's a difficulty. Changing your language is a very powerful way of opening up the mind to new ideas. Instead of 'why', ask how is it that my mind chooses to think this way?!

☐ **Task:** Having considered your perception of yourself as a rider, ask yourself questions such as:

- When does this happen, specifically
- What are you thinking before this happens, specifically?
- Where are you riding, specifically?
- Does this *always* happen?! *Every* time you ride?
- How are you riding when you feel this way?
- What specific evidence do you have that you're not riding well throughout this?
- What are you not doing when it all goes right?
- What are you not doing when it all goes wrong?
- What would happen exactly if you didn't feel/ride this way?
- How do you know they're thinking that?
- How do you know your horse thinks like that?
- Think of some other questions to recover a broader perspective on your riding.

Perception is projection

In simple terms, perception is projection means that what we see in others, is something we see in ourselves. Think of it as a reflection of some part of us. If our perception of someone is that they are arrogant, what we are actually doing, inside our head, is having our own arrogance reflect back on us! The unconscious mind, as we will see, takes everything personally; calling someone else arrogant is, in effect, the same as telling yourself that you're arrogant. This is why riders who are overly critical of others, suffer the consequences of perception is projection: the criticisms they make are the characteristics they have inside themselves too. They are telling themselves about their own faults. This reinforces the negative criticism inside their mind and the unconscious mind believes it to be unswervingly true.

Challenge yourself to refrain from being overly critical of others, use positive criticism and break the habit of gossiping, this too is taken personally by the unconscious mind.

Perception is projection can work by a second means. Often, we unconsciously project onto others how we think they will behave. This is true of how we think about our horses. The unconscious mind, ever the loyal servant, endeavours to make our projection real. For example, we may unknowingly project onto our horse that hacking down the lanes is nerve-wracking. The horse's own sensory perception, working at a higher level than a human's, is able to detect this. The horse becomes wary and on heightened alert, ready to spook or bolt at the sight of a plastic bag or wheelie bin.

Be mindful of what you are projecting onto your horse. Clear your mind using the techniques described in this book. As we shall see later, 'Hakalau' (Chapter 8) is particularly good to use in the moments when such thoughts pop into our head and when we are riding.

Are you 'at cause' or 'at effect'?

How would it be to take responsibility and be in control of your riding success? Not to have to pin failure or disappointment on any other person or horse, weather forecasts or prevailing conditions?! Wouldn't that be a relief?

You are said to be 'at cause' if you are

- responsible for all you actions, past, present and future
- with no attachment of blame to yourself or others (playing the blame game, that's called being at effect)

Imagine that you are given the gift of knowing everything that has ever happened to you, and what is happening to you right now, is your responsibility. Just imagine that for a moment. Try that feeling on.

Now try this one: you're to blame for everything that has ever happened to you and what is happening to you.

The two should feel entirely different, the first being rather more upbeat than the second!

Taking responsibility for all your actions empowers you, because it gives you a feeling that you're in charge and makes you feel like you have choices.

You are at 'effect' if

- you reject your responsibility for your riding
- you blame others or make excuses
- you feel disempowered or disconnected
- you feel trapped, that you have no other choices

Consider this: when you're a very old lady/old man, how important will that blame and those excuses be?!

☐ **Task:** Try this at work, at home and around your stables, yard or barn. Try it for a week and then review the changes you've made

1. Be aware of each time you complain about something. Count up your complaints for a whole day, then a whole week. You'll be surprised how much we all complain. Complaints are the domain of being at effect.
2. Notice how much others complain too. How many people around you, your friends, family, neighbours and fellow riders spend chunks of their time complaining?!
3. Be aware of how much society and the media encourages being at effect e.g.,

    - Mention of financial **crisis** (the media relish a recession) – does it mean that we all have to feel that our own finances are controlled by others?
    - Mention of any bad or negative state of affairs (the media love to put a negative spin on news items) – does that mean our own personal world is an unhappy place that we have no say in?
    - Mention of seasonal weather and all the associated downsides – does it really mean there's danger all around?

☐ **Task:** Now that you're aware of all the moaning around you, become resilient to those people who are at effect. Keep at cause by choosing your riding companions and those whom you chat to with care. Remove yourself from those who sap your energy, spend minimal time with the at effect brigade!

In starting to be at cause, we start to see results faster! You are responsible for your results and that should be a liberating announcement!

☐ **Task:** Assume that you are the equal in your relationship with your horse. You are responsible for the connection with your horse and it's up to you to be responsible, fair and assertive. Think of it as your job as a rider. If you've previously allowed your horse to lead, this shift in dynamics can be over-turned more quickly than you think and will enhance the harmony in the connection.

Your personal history

When riders seek help from NLP Practitioners or hypnotherapists, they are often asked a series of questions. These provide insight and can illuminate the areas outside the awareness of the rider, which are leading to problems when riding. Answer the questions using the first words or phrases that enter your head. Cogitation and rumination will likely produce an answer from your logical (conscious mind), rather than the part of the mind we want to change (the unconscious mind). If an answer about your confidence doesn't spring to mind, don't force it, move on to the next question. We build a problem up in our mind using words to describe it; if we start to stumble over the words, it means the issue is starting to loosen. Let's not tighten it again!

Remember to jot down your answers in a journal or notebook.

1. List your major issue(s).
2. For each issue, take out the most emotionally 'charged' word, the one that evokes emotion the most. Automatically write down the meaning of that word *to you*.
3. Now look at your meaning(s). Take out the most emotionally 'charged' word, the one that evokes emotion the most. Automatically write down the meaning of that word *to you*.
4. Ask yourself now, what's your confidence issue?
5. How do you know your issue is a problem?
6. When don't you do the problem?
7. What are you not deciding when you don't do the problem?
8. What obstacles do you face because of this problem?
9. Would you class yourself as a nervous rider?
10. If you answered yes to the above, ask yourself, "Is that all I am? Aren't I much more than that?" (Think about any area of your life). If you find this question difficult, think what your best friend or your horse would say about you!
11. Consider your answer to (a) above. And, aren't you much more than that even? How do you know?
12. If you could wish to be, do or have something, what would it be?
13. All of my life, I ………….
14. I get nervous thinking about………………
15. I am a person who…………………..
16. What behaviours get in the way of your happiness on your horse?
17. What would you like to start doing?
18. What would you like to stop doing?
19. What would you like to do more of? What would you like to do less of?
20. What are the things you feel you should, can, and must do?
21. What motivates you?

22. What has this question set unearthed for you?

R,R&R Chapter 1

Working with the unconscious mind can be tiring, initially. Just like anyone who starts a new exercise regime, working unfamiliar muscles, you need time to rest! Take some time, a day or two, to **reflect, rest and relax**. Take the time to slow down, release any pressure valves and kick back. This may feel like you're standing still, but paradoxically, slowing down and taking time to digest is a valuable means of moving forwards more quickly!

Think about the major themes of this chapter and how they apply to you. After your R,R&R, put the ideas to the test , enjoy, have fun and think of this as a game. Are you ready to be in the game? Here's a quick summary of Chapter 1.

- Our minds filter out almost all the information we receive from the external world, we only have a fickle grasp of reality!
- Listen out for times when you distort, delete and generalise information.
- Perception is projection – riders who are overly critical of others are demonstrating that those characteristics are part of them too!
- Project onto other people and your horse, the thoughts you'd like reflected back to you.
- Being at cause means taking responsibility and empowers you to feel that you're in charge and have choices.
- Completing a personal history can be very illuminating!

Chapter 1 – What did you learn? How will you use this to boost your riding confidence?

2. A tour of the conscious and unconscious minds

Introduction

Your conscious mind is everything you are aware of at the present moment. Conscious thoughts tend to be intentional, controllable, serial in nature (i.e. step-by-step) and relatively easy to put into words. You are using your conscious mind to read these words. As you read, you make a meaningful set of ideas from the text; you make a logical understanding of how the words relate to you. When you are thinking about your riding, you can reason very logically why there is no need to be fearful! You may have a good independent seat, be confident around horses and have sufficient expertise to ride safely and securely. Having such logical thoughts, however, even using them as affirmations or mantras, is often of limited benefit when you find yourself anxious when *doing* the very thing that scares you. What's needed is more conscious-unconscious mind agreement, as we will see.

There is nothing woolly or fanciful about the unconscious mind. In NLP, the unconscious mind represents everything you're not currently aware of thinking. Unconscious thoughts can be recalled and brought into the conscious mind quite effortlessly. For example, you probably weren't thinking about your phone number, but if you need to, you can recite it and bring it into your conscious mind. Rest assured that everything you have ever learned is stored in your unconscious mind, as too are all the ways in which you can improve your riding confidence. The knowledge may not be as easily accessible as your phone number right now, it is, however it is accessible using techniques such as NLP or hypnotherapy.

(Note: some branches of psychology use the term 'subconscious' too. In NLP, however, we tend to avoid the use of this word, because it has connotations of a mind of lower importance, a sub-level below the conscious mind. As we will see, nothing could be further from the truth!)

To help us understand the enormous significance of the unconscious, Sigmund Freud used an iceberg metaphor. Just as the tip of an iceberg floats above the surface, the conscious mind is what we are aware of at the surface level. Whereas the huge mass that remains below, the unconscious mind, is the largest and most influential part. It is by changing the thought processes of this part of the mind, that we can overcome our fears and anxieties in our riding.

It is sometimes quite amusing to think how self important the conscious mind thinks it is. The logical mind thinks it's the all-important CEO of us and that the unconscious mind is little more than the boiler operator making sure that our body keeps going. The summary below shows you how vastly more important that our unconscious mind really is.

Summary

The conscious mind

- Reservoir of short-term memory, logic and analysis
- Controls 3% of your behaviour and actions
- Free will lies here
- Impulses travel at 200 km per second
- It is the 'goal setter' – it analyses what you want and puts it into words

The unconscious mind

- Reservoir of emotions, habits and memories
- Controls 97% of your behaviour and actions
- Averages 10 billion actions per second
- Impulses travel at 160,000 km per second
- It is the 'goal getter' – it takes the information you supply about what you want and makes associations that become opportunities to reach your goal

☐ **Task:** In your own words, describe the conscious and unconscious minds

The major roles of the unconscious mind

1. It is where the emotions are housed. This is of great importance to us as riders, imagine being able to choose your emotional state, anytime or anywhere. Wouldn't that be useful?! We'll talk about controlling our state of mind in later chapters, for now remember that it's *your* mind and, given practice, *you* can control *your* state.

2. It stores and organises the memories, rather like we store files in folders on a computer hard drive. You could search for your files by date or by name, this is also how we access our memories. Memories are more vivid if we link significant emotions to them. In other words, we can charge an unpleasant memory and/or blow it up out of all proportion simply by adding negative emotions to it. The more emotions we layer onto the memory, the more prevailing it becomes. Think of a time when you were happy as a rider,

think of a specific time, do you have a picture? And as you picture yourself now, do the emotions come flooding back?

It's not recommended that you remember unhappier moments, as this can reinforce the memory and the emotions. However, by removing the negative emotions associated with that memory, we can clean up our unconscious mind and learn from the memory; then the memory aids our development, rather than hinders it.

3. It can repress painful memories and present them at a later date for us to resolve. Do you ever wish a memory would just go away, stop entering your head at the worst possible moment? By popping that memory into your mind, the unconscious mind is actually telling you to deal with that memory, sort out what needs to be done to move on.

4. It generates habits for us. This can be a huge aid to us – it saves an enormous amount of energy that we would otherwise expend in having to think through our every action. For example, if you drive, you may understand how automatic that can be – you know when to brake or change gear, slow down or speed up. Those learnt behaviours are done largely without too much conscious thought. However, unhelpful habits, such as the seemingly automatic triggering of nerves, need to be re-thought out and new strategies introduced. Importantly, our horse's unconscious mind will develop habits in a similar fashion. If you become anxious when you see a particular jump or before you strike off into canter, you horse will pick up on this and a vicious circle will ensue. Being aware of this can make us more determined as riders to avoid creating unhelpful habits in the first place.

What to do: stop analysing past events. Stop describing them in immense detail with others or writing them in social media posts, this reinforces the memory and **your unconscious mind does not know if it is really happening or is a memory**. Be brief in your descriptions of these types of events if you have to talk or write about them at all.

If your mind conjures up a 'what if' scenario, forcibly create a happy ending or clear your screen in your mind's eye or use 'Pattern Interrupt'. Pattern interrupt is rather like when we see our horse about to escape out of the stable or when you see a child about to leap off a big stack of hay bales onto the concrete floor. We quickly, and with authority, say something like "NO! NO!!". Or when a negative thought tries to surface, my personal favourite is, "DELETE! DELETE!! DELETE!!!"

Other pattern interrupts are useful. If used early enough and often enough, the interruption becomes part of a new habit.

- Undo the negative language: "That was how the *old* me thought," or "I *used* to be like that."

- Sing!! Have your favourite song in repeat mode running through your mind
- Recite your least favourite times table!
- If the 'what ifs' are more your own inner voice, rather than images, change that voice to Donald Duck's!

5. The unconscious mind is highly symbolic, this means that it is very much the realm of pictures, imagination and dreams. It does not process words as easily as the conscious mind, this is why positive affirmations often have some, but limited, success: they are said very consciously, often without engaging the unconscious mind fully. That said, the unconscious mind does enjoy communication with the conscious mind via the imagination. Using the imagination is incredibly powerful, as it is by this means that we can transmit and receive information between our two minds. Now we have an effortless way of talking to the unconscious: use your imagination to suggest what you want and the unconscious will work to make it happen. The suggestions can be feelings, sounds, pictures or your own self-talk; adjust the picture you have like you would adjust your television to make it the best picture and sound quality ever! Adding in positive feelings seals the ideas in our minds. Interestingly, the unconscious mind cannot distinguish between real and imagined memories. This makes it more straightforward to insert that compelling picture into the unconscious mind. We'll make use of this in later techniques. Professional riders as well as athletes commonly use mental images to rehearse the successful completion of their competition. Practise visualisation often, it's as necessary as physical preparation for success.

   What to do: if your mind plagues you with 'what ifs', make sure you use one or more of the Pattern Interrupt techniques to remove them.

6. The unconscious mind prefers the path of least resistance, i.e., it takes the easiest option. When presented with two possible outcomes, one of fear and anxiety, beating ourselves up and feeling generally miserable about our riding, the other, enjoying working with our horse, celebrating small victories and learning from errors: which do you think your unconscious would take? It's actually less-energy sapping to ensure a positive outcome. Sometimes the unconscious has not been offered a choice, hence, the more attractive scenario does not transpire. As nervous riders, people are sometimes frozen into tunnelled vision and the unconscious mind thinks there is only one choice: people think if they bang their head enough times against that brick wall, something magical will happen!

What to do: try this visualisation, to open the unconscious mind to the possibility of options

- Think about your riding issue now, think about when you first started to feel that way. We could say 'when' you decided to feel that way…..do you have a picture?
- Where were you when your mind decided to make feel this way?
- Just before your mind made that decision to feel nervous, where were you? (think of this as going back in time when there were no nerves about the current riding issue). Do you have a picture of this time?
- Looking at your picture, imagine standing at a crossroads and opening up before you as 5,10 or 20 roads, each a separate roadway to your future. Some roads would lead to a future you wouldn't want – selling your horse and tack; not riding, paying someone else to ride……other roads require some mind work, but possible, e.g., using the techniques in this book to overcome your nerves……one of the roads is the one you actually took to get to the present time……
- Which road would you take now? Notice how it feels to have more choices…
- NOW, as you think about your present situation, notice how many roads you have at this crossroads you have…how many options to do things differently now?
- Think of that problem and notice how you feel now
- As you think about the next time you want to ride/compete, knowing what you know now, notice how much better you feel

7. The unconscious mind takes everything very personally and is listening in all the time. As riders we criticise ourselves for the slightest mistake, analysing our 'failures' and having little time for self-praise. We treat ourselves very badly, unaware of the harm it causes. The unconscious mind, having been told by you that you aren't good enough or worthy enough as a rider, has taken your spoken and unspoken words to heart and now believes you in the most literal sense. The unconscious mind is not a literary type, we could describe it more like a 5-year-old child in this respect. Would you verbally chastise a child in the same way you chastise yourself? How harmful would that be? Day after day? How would that child ever become a happy, contented rider? Take care also when talking about others, as the unconscious mind thinks you are talking about yourself. Be kind in all that you say and think about others and, if you really can't be kind about them, say and think neutral thoughts!

What to do: speak kindly about yourself and others. Remove yourself from all types of gossip, complaints, moans and groans. Practise at work, at home and at the yard. It's not an easy task, but it works wonders for your mental mind muscles.

8. It does not understand negatives such as 'not', 'never', 'no-one/nowhere/nothing'. This means it ignores those words. We really need to reflect on our language, particularly our self-talk. Before a ride or competition, do you ever find yourself saying that you don't want to fall off or have the horse refuse or some other similar event happen? What you say may be, "I do *not* want X to happen," what your unconscious mind hears is, "I do want X to happen." It simply ignores the word 'not'. E.g., "I don't want my horse to refuse that jump," your mind hears, "I do want my horse to refuse that jump." Your unconscious mind will search for ways to make your thoughts happen for you, so take care!

    What to do: tell your unconscious mind what you *want*, not what you don't want. We're so used to listing all the things we don't want to happen, we forget the things we do. Take care when you hear yourself use the word 'not' or 'don't' and re-phrase it quickly in your head. This may seem like a small thing to do, but the changes inside your head can be huge. Practise saying what you want (rather than what you don't want) from colleagues, family, friends and notice the effect your words have on them!

9. It controls bodily functions automatically, regulating and maintaining the integrity of the body. Something to think about: when you feel nervous, do the physical symptoms heighten your awareness of the fear? Which came first, the idea of being frightened or the physical feelings of fear? Tony Robbins says that physiology changes psychology.

    What to do: Move your body more, go for a invigorating walk or run, get some fresh air. Even briskly sweeping the yard can divert nervous energy into physical energy and release the tension.

10. Is there to serve and protect you. Very often the thing we most want to do and enjoy is the thing that frightens us. This is confuses the unconscious mind. Many thousands of years ago, the unconscious mind served our cavemen ancestors as a protective mechanism to remove them from danger: the flight or fright response. We may consider ourselves more sophisticated than cavemen, yet our unconscious mind functions in much the same way, it will strive to keep us from harm. If we communicate to our unconscious that riding is somehow frightening, the unconscious will work to remove us from that danger. It may stimulate the outpouring of the hormones adrenaline and noradrenaline, causing us to feel the full force of anxiety and fear. The shaking hands and jelly-legs, the butterflies, the inability to talk or think straight, the pounding heartbeat and nausea all serve to prevent us getting on the horse, the 'danger' we have told our unconscious mind about on a daily basis. The same 'danger' we have told our unconscious mind that we are inadequate to face. The unconscious mind is trying to make us run from the 'danger' and be safe once more. It is trying to prevent us from riding!

    What to do: we need to reinforce to the unconscious mind that all is well. Take a deep breath in and slowly exhale. Be aware of your breathing. Now, in time to your breathing, say, "I'm safe now.....and now......and now......" This gives your conscious mind something to do (saying something and thinking about breathing), and conveys to your unconscious mind that you want to do this.

11. It generates, stores and distributes energy throughout the body. It is valuable to know that negative emotions and memories require considerable energy to maintain. Running and maintaining disaster movies in our mind for example can be energetically costly. Removing the negative emotions leaves us feeling far lighter and energised to do what we want to do.

    What to do: See the Fast Phobia Method (Chapter 6) or investigate techniques such as Time Line Therapy™ which release such energy, for more information see http://www.traceycolenlp.com/timeline-therapy/time-line-therapy-for-equestrians/

12. It works best as an integrated unit, together with the conscious mind. This means that when both parts of the mind are in agreement, there is a certain ease and flow in our actions. Think about something you do well, without really trying. Maybe you drive well or you're good at your job, maybe you can sew or speed read. Whatever it is, it means your unconscious and conscious minds are working together. Think about a rider you know who does not suffer from nerves. All that's happening in their mind is that their conscious-unconscious connection is congruent with what they are doing. When your conscious and unconscious are focused on the same aim, goals are more easily achieved. Conflicts between our conscious and unconscious minds can block negative and destructive behaviours being resolved. Have you ever thought that you could ride the way you want to and then within seconds, had the opposite thought? "I know I'm a good enough rider to do X, but I get nervous when I think about doing X." Having push-pull thoughts is known as incongruence and it is another way that we become drained of energy, motivation and determination to ride how we know we can.

    What to do: to remove that feeling of push-pull, as soon as a negative thought hits you, say to yourself, "DELETE, DELETE, DELETE!" or, "That's how I USED to think, that's the OLD me."

Self-sabotage

By reading through the functions of the unconscious mind, you may have been alerted to the fact that in many instances we sabotage our own riding enjoyment. Although the unconscious mind works tirelessly to guard your wellbeing, it is working under your orders and taking them literally. This is why negative outcomes can continue in riders who don't take charge and change their thinking. "If you do what you've always done, you'll get what you've always gotten." -Tony Robbins

The importance of practising

Having an unconscious mind receptive to change takes some concerted effort in choosing our words with care. Practise removing negative thoughts and what ifs, as well as gossip and complaining from your mind. This is akin to a good spring-clean and prepares the mind for change. Don't skip this vital preparation stage, as these are foundations that will secure your confidence.

☐ **Task:** Write down your own riding experiences, being aware of how the unconscious mind works is the first step to change! Think of the way the unconscious mind was operating on an unhelpful setting and may need to go back to the factory default setting.

Did you complete the task? If you completed it, then great, you're on your way to being consciously aware of changes that you can make quite easily to break down your problem areas. If you didn't do the task, do you feel a little guilty or left out or are you just wanting to get to the nub of NLP, without doing the work? Unfortunately, as with most new learning, we need to create a rock-solid foundation to be able to scaffold more and more complex thoughts and ideas on to.

R,R&R Chapter 2

It's time once again to slow things down, stop for a little **reflection, rest and relaxation.** Remember this R, R & R is important mind work too! Here is a quick summary of Chapter 2.

- The conscious mind is logical and analytical and thinks it's in charge. However, it is only 3% of your behaviours and actions.
- The unconscious mind is the other 97%.
- The unconscious mind stores the emotions, memories and generates our habits.
- The unconscious mind takes everything very personally and is always listening into our conversations and thoughts.
- The unconscious mind likes to serve, but it needs very clear instructions, preferably in visualisations or positive, unambiguous language.
- Focus on what you want, as the unconscious mind does not 'hear' the word 'not'.
- Self-sabotage is what happens when we (unintentionally) work against the unconscious mind.

Chapter 2 - What did you learn? How will you use this to boost your riding confidence?

3. Beliefs

By first recognising a limiting belief we can start to eliminate it. Sometimes these beliefs are so embedded in the mind we don't even know they're there! In some branches of psychology, it is thought that our true nature as humans is to be happy. Anything that gets in the way and blocks this happiness is a limiting belief of some sort. Let's examine what (limiting) beliefs mean for riders.

A belief is the acceptance of something as true. It can also be thinking that something could be true. Beliefs are judgments and evaluations we make about others and ourselves. Your beliefs stem from your collection of experiences and are stored in your unconscious mind. This means that they are often outside of our conscious awareness and you may not even 'know' you have them! Your beliefs may not make logical sense. Making sense and being rational is the province of the conscious mind. How many times have you had an argument or discussion and just known you were right, but had little evidence to base your argument on?

Your beliefs and ideas are what set you apart, they make you, you. They can be tremendously empowering and useful in our daily lives as well as in our overall way of being; they can be limiting and restrict us and prevent us being open to new possibilities. Unfortunately, some beliefs about ourselves can interfere with our potential to excel and lead to us never starting a new project or abandoning an idea before giving ourselves a chance. This type of belief is known as a limiting belief, they are often unhelpful, unhealthy or even damaging to confidence levels.

Anything that is at odds with your beliefs, limiting or limitless, quite literally does not enter your head: your unconscious mind filters those things out. Beliefs are one of the filters in the NLP Communication Model (see Chapter 1). If you don't believe that you can ride the way you want to, anything you see, feel or hear will demonstrate this to you. All other information to the contrary has been neatly filtered out. Thus proving you right! The 'evidence' that tells you that you can't ride the way you want to, is the result of an intricate filtering mechanism; it is not the whole story.

Limiting beliefs

Below is a list of limiting beliefs commonly held by riders. You may identify with some or most of them. The list is not exhaustive, you may want to add your own favourite, even unique ones!

- I'm not a good enough rider to do X

- I would be a better rider if I had a better horse
- I don't have any natural ability
- I wish I could do X (a yearning of sorts)
- I'm not good enough to compete
- None of the people on my yard compete, so I can't do it either
- If I ride down that lane, my horse will spook and I'll fall off
- I can't canter
- I can't mount unless I use my own mounting block
- If I did compete, I'd probably fall off or make a fool of myself
- When people watch me ride, they think I'm not good enough for my horse/I can't ride/I don't deserve such a great horse
- I can't ride well when people watch me
- I can't ride well
- When people on my yard hear that I've entered a competition, they'll laugh at me
- People on my yard think I'm a hopeless rider
- People on my yard are always talking about my riding behind my back
- I don't deserve my horse
- My horse is too good for me, s/he needs a better rider
- I can't jump verticals/oxers/jumps with fillers/that silly filler/water trays
- I can't ride when it's windy/rainy/sunny
- My horse doesn't like it when I ask for canter
- My horse won't canter steadily on grass
- My horse doesn't like red jumps
- My horse doesn't like to be ridden early in the day/late in the day
- If I bought a new X for my horse, I'd be able to ride better
- If I bought a new X for myself, I'd be able to ride better
- Everyone else can ride my horse better than me
- I doubt my ability
- My instructor/trainer says I'm a good rider, but s/he's just saying that to make me feel better

Think about these:

- Did you ever have trouble getting beyond a certain level in your riding?

- Do you ever feel like you're in a vicious circle and history repeats itself (maybe through different horses, different yards, different instructors)?
- Do you ever feel unhappy and uninspired about your riding?
- Do you ever feel stuck with no options?
- Are you fed up at home or work or with your riding?
- Does your confidence sometimes falter in certain situations and not in others (e.g., you are confident in your career, which can be demanding and require you to be on top of your game, but then lose confidence riding)?
- Is your riding anxiety only triggered in certain situations?

Which ones struck a chord with you? Add your own limiting beliefs, if any.

Now, as you think about your riding issues, can you identify your major limiting beliefs. Highlight or underline all those that apply.

☐ **Task:** Look over all the statements of limiting beliefs that apply to you. What beliefs about yourself have you discovered? Choose the one(s) that stand(s) out for you. Write it/them down.

We are going to try to tease out some of your unconscious limiting beliefs. When we think about a root cause of a belief, we have 3 types:

a) Feeling helpless
b) Feeling hopeless
c) Feeling worthless

1. Helpless
    - Why does this always happen to me?
    - Riding is a rich person's game
    - I always attract the wrong people
    - I just can't change
    - I always get it wrong

2. Hopeless
    - Somethings will never change
    - There's no point trying

- It will never work
- I will never be able to do that
- I never have any luck
- I'm no good at X

3. Worthless
- I don't deserve it
- I'm not good enough and I never will be
- I have no confidence
- People say I'm useless
- I think I'm useless

Remember: by saying and thinking such limiting statements, we are reinforcing the ideas that are preventing us from improving and progressing! The language we use is often limiting and it gives a certain power to the beliefs.

"Whether you think you can or think you can't, you're right" – Henry Ford.

The good news is that just as we use language to create and maintain these beliefs, we can use language to unravel and eliminate them too.

☐ **Task:** Look at the statements you wrote down in the last task. Ask yourself the following questions and write down the first answer that comes into your head. It may be a sentence, a word or a picture. Don't over analyse: just write down the first association, otherwise your answers will be too 'conscious mind'. Don't worry if you think it is the wrong answer: whatever you say will be perfect for you.

1. What must be true...
2. What else must...
3. I have this lim...
4. What does that mea...
5. How is that true for you?
6. How is that a problem for you?
7. What did you make that mean about...

Repeat this task for any other statements of limiting beliefs

You may well find that you discover a 'rule' that you may not have known existed. This can be very insightful. If you missed this part out, wanting to gallop through the basics, go back now, write down your answers and complete the task. It really is important that you discover all the ways your own mind works. This is incredibly empowering!

Many statements fit the pattern of:

- I can….I cannot (impossibility)
- I must…..I must not (necessity)
- I should…..I should not (necessity)

They can be distilled into sentences of two types:

1. 'I'm too X'
2. 'Whenever X happens, I respond by doing Y'.

☐ **Task:** Write down a short version of your limiting belief(s). You have finished when you have a short, simple statement that will cause you to experience what you do in terms of your riding.

☐ **Task:** Now distill that statement down to fit into one or both of these patterns:

- I'm too X
- Whenever X happens, I respond by doing Y

In the next chapter, we'll discover how to break down and eliminate these limiting beliefs. Being able to remove a limiting belief is incredibly empowering. There is nothing to stop you being the person you want to be, having what you want to have or doing what you want to do, other than the belief that it is possible. Ask yourself very firmly: "What stops me?" This is a powerful trigger question to access your limiting belief. Now we can start working to eliminate it!

R,R&R Chapter 2

Take some time now for your **refection, rest and relaxation**. This is a time to step back, think about the limiting beliefs that you knew you had and those that you didn't! Were they all riding-related? Do they all have an impact on your riding? Here's a quick summary of Chapter 3.

- Anything that is at odds with your beliefs, limiting or limitless, quite literally does not enter your head: your unconscious mind filters those things out. If you don't believe that you can ride the way you want to, anything you see, feel or hear will conspire to demonstrate this to you.
- When we think about a root cause of a belief, we have 3 types:

    a) Feeling helpless
    b) Feeling hopeless
    c) Feeling worthless

- The good news is that just as we use language to support and maintain these beliefs, we can use language to unravel and eliminate them too.
- You may well find that you discover a 'rule' that you may not have known existed.
- Ask yourself very firmly: "What stops me?" This is a powerful trigger question to access your limiting belief.

Chapter 3 – What did you learn? How will you use this to boost your riding confidence?

4. Removing limiting beliefs

Beliefs, as you now know, are a result of experiences. The content of an experience, however, is whatever you choose to focus on. The meaning of the experience can be whatever you want it to be. Sometimes, the meaning we take from an experience is not a positive one, so our meaning needs a little re-phrasing to make it more useful to us. In NLP, this is known as reframing. For example, looking back at a dramatic experience from long ago may make you laugh now, although it was far from funny at the time. Your mind has reframed this event, so you see it from a different point of view now. By changing a setting or context of an idea, we can change its meaning. For instance, if your horse is on strict box rest, with limited time out of the stable, you could choose to see this is as a heavy burden of keeping him/her occupied and dreading every day at the yard. Alternatively, you could choose to see it as an opportunity to do some extra grooming or learning about basic horse massage. It's the same scenario, with two very different viewpoints. This is how we shift our perception of limiting ideas and beliefs.

There are two types of reframes, the context reframe and the meaning reframe. Both work well when humour, positivity and creativity are applied! Think about why jokes work, there is often a sudden change in meaning or context that makes us laugh. Think about how politicians can make an economic downturn sound like a walk in the park! They can use spin (reframe) to eke out a positive statement in the face of a glaringly negative situation.

Review your limiting beliefs from the previous chapter and decide whether they fit into the pattern of 'I'm too X' (use a context reframe) or 'Whenever X happens, I respond by doing Y' (use a meaning reframe).

1. Context reframe - a different point of view

This works well for limiting beliefs and other situations where you find yourself saying "I'm too X". Looking at a limiting belief from a different perspective can help you stay calm and reduce your stress level. Opening your mind to other possibilities, rather than the worse case scenario is the secret to context reframing.

☐ **Task:** Example: I'm too scared to canter (this is usually a fear of speed or feeling of being out of control)

I have a good, secure seat and I know how to control a horse's speed. I also know that a canter is not necessarily faster than a trot, it is just a different rhythm. If I keep the horse between my hands and legs, keep the canter slow, I will be in control.

Now reframe your limiting belief!

2. Meaning reframe – changing a negative into a positive

This works well for statements of the type, "Whenever X happens, I respond by doing Y". These limiting beliefs require that we turn a negative into a positive and often arise when we have already had something go wrong ourselves or are conscious of someone else having had a bad experience. Because you had a bad experience you might have framed all your riding issues as negative. To reframe, you need to imagine a time in your past when you actually had fun riding or competing or doing what you most want to do now. Recalling such events will help you to associate the idea to a positive experience rather than a negative one. You can no longer say that "Whenever X happens, I respond Y," because that hasn't always been so. Alternatively, think about how to change your response: are you riding a different horse? Do you have lessons/training sessions now? What did you learn from your past experience that has made you change in a positive way now?

☐ **Task:** Example: Whenever I compete, I get so nervous that I'm disappointed with the result

Being nervous causes me to ride differently and I don't perform as well as I can. Being nervous does not serve me; it makes things harder. I know that in a situation where I need to act fast to stay on or get my horse over a jump, I do the corrective action instinctively, I don't need to think. I don't have time to be scared. I just do it. So being nervous when everything is ok makes no sense. It just doesn't help me in any way. I don't need the nerves to be 'sharp', I can be sharp whenever I need to be. I can choose to be nervous or not. I choose to be confident!

Now reframe your limiting belief!

It will take some practice to become aware of a limiting belief and then reframe it into something positive. Like any behaviour, practice makes perfect. This may not happen overnight or may not happen the very first time you reframe. You will, however, start to reframe more easily and consequently, you will reframe more effectively. You may start to encounter new limiting beliefs, so be aware of the helpless/hopeless/unworthy statements creeping in again.

☐ **Task:** Practise this other language trick and I'll reveal its importance at the end

The key here is to write down the 3 steps in terms of what words you would use. When you have the 3 sentences, read them **out loud** (preferably) five times quickly. When you have finished, ask yourself, "So what was that old problem?"

1. Think about the current riding problem now. Do you have a picture in your mind? Be riding in the picture, so you can see your horse's neck etc. (you are not watching yourself, but doing the actions). Feel how it is to have that problem. Say to yourself, "When I think about how I used to ride in the past, I felt……" (Notice that we've put this into the past tense to convince the unconscious mind that it *is* in the past.)
2. As you think about yourself in this moment, step out of the picture you have in your mind and watch yourself riding. Say to yourself in the present moment, "If I'm gong to change, I need to put these mind techniques into practise."
3. Now, step into a future picture and ride at your best. Be riding in the picture, so you can see your horse's neck etc. (you are not watching yourself, but doing the actions). Say to yourself, "In using and practising mind techniques, I was able to see/feel that……".

For Step 3, insert empowering beliefs that you want to have instead of your old ones. Use empowering beliefs that evoke feelings of possibility and probability. Here are some examples for you to try on and see how they feel/sound:

- I deserve …..
- Riding/competing/jumping/cantering is easy for me
- I feel supported in having what I want
- I'm worthy of this challenge
- I've got what it takes to be a good rider/competitor
- I enjoy all aspects of my riding
- I look forward to ….
- I feel safe and secure in the knowledge that I'm a good rider
- I view my riding as really fun
- Riding gives me a sense of freedom
- When I ride I know I have all the skill I need to feel in control
- I am open to seeing things differently and trying new things

- I can achieve whatever I set my mind to
- I love learning new ways of thinking about my riding
- I know my unconscious mind will look after me in a way that enables me to ride and compete at my best

This language pattern helps to shift the balance of believing in your limiting belief in favour of breaking it down. Not sure? If you did the exercise out loud, when you came to answer, "So what was the old problem?" did you stumble or hesitate over the wording? Problems, as we shall see in Chapter 5 have a thick boundary around them, this boundary is made up of our words and descriptions. Cut through the words and we blow the problem apart. If you can't express your problem eloquently, then it's already breaking up!

Questioning your limiting belief

This exercise is shaking up the belief, so that your mind's grip on it loosens. Sometimes, asking your unconscious mind a question about your limiting belief(s) helps to bring those deepest beliefs to the surface, ready to be dealt with in the next chapters.

1. As you think of that riding issue, do you have a picture? Imagine stepping back into your body there. Notice what you see through your own eyes, what you hear and what you feel. Be aware of how you are deciding what actions to take.
2. If there were a statement (it could be a question) that guided or triggered your limited thinking, what would it be?
3. Now think of that statement. Does that statement remind you of the situation? Does it feel the same? As you say that statement or question to yourself, does your picture stay the same? Are the sounds the same? If not, ask your unconscious mind for the statement that is guiding you to this unwanted belief and behaviour.
4. If you were to know, what is your unconscious mind's **positive** intention in this statement? If you receive a negative intention, reframe by asking, "What does that get for me that's really positive?" Your mind will have a positive intention for making you feel nervous. It may be something like the mind wants to protect you. It may be completely different!
5. If you find that your mind gives you a word like 'protection' or 'safety'. Say to yourself "I am protected, now I want to be X when I ride" or "I am safe already. Now I want to be X when I ride"
6. Check you have the best statement to help you understand and eliminate your limiting belief. Is there a statement that would be more effective in getting you the positive benefits you want?
7. Now step back into your body in that riding situation and say the statement to yourself - say it out loud, as you imagine being in that situation. Notice that when you're in that situation now, a new statement is quietly at the back of your mind, guiding your behaviour, and check that that feels much more enjoyable! Imagine a future time, when you'll be in that situation again and check how saying the new statement changes the way you feel.

What if it doesn't work?

First of all, being aware of your limiting belief goes a long way to eliminating it: beliefs that were previously unconscious or that changed during the process are now ready to be removed. In place of the limiting belief, insert new, compelling and empowering beliefs. Question your beliefs and believe in the answers (if you have found yourself unsure of whether or not to believe that your unconscious mind can communicate with you, then this is a limiting belief: it needs to be eliminated too!) Make sure that you have practised this over and over and set yourself new reframes that resonate with *you*. Remember too that *your* beliefs can be changed, but only if you want them to change and only if *you* change them! When you think of a limiting belief, make sure it's all about you, not your horse, not the people on your yard or your instructor.

More change work – using visualisations

Visualisation is incredibly effective. Having the ability to show your unconscious mind what your goal is in images, with sounds, voices and feelings adds depth to your desirable outcome is of great value. The unconscious mind revels in this type of communication, as opposed to words and prose.

☐ **Task:** Only attempt this if you have full, painless movement in your shoulder, neck and arm!

1. Lift one of your arms out to the side, so that it is in line with your shoulder and parallel to the floor. Point your index finger and keep your arm straight. Now, without rotating your body, move your arm backwards so that your finger is pointing behind you. Stretch so that you are as far behind you as you can go. Turn your head and make a mental note of where your finger is pointing.
2. Relax your arm. Close your eyes. Imagine seeing and feeling the same exercise as the one above. Visualise how far your arm reached behind you. Now visualize reaching even further behind you. A couple of centimetres or more if you can.
3. Repeat step 1. Note where you finger is pointing
4. Did you move around further after the visualisation? If so, then you know how to communicate with your unconscious mind using pictures! If not, try the task again, concentrating in your visualisation on moving that arm further.
5. Reflect how this simple visualisation improved your ability to do the exercise. Consider how this could improve your riding confidence and riding skills!

By now, you should have loosened up some, if not all of your limiting beliefs and have noticed that your perspective on your reality is changing. We can shake up your negative thoughts and beliefs even more!

Changing a limiting belief using a 4-way visualisation

This technique involves a series of 4 pictures as seen in your mind's eye. We will exchange the characteristics of your picture of your current issue with a picture that represents something that is no longer true. Hence, you mind will consider your riding issues as no longer true.

Then we'll exchange a picture of your ideal ride with the characteristics of a picture that is always true. And ta-da, your mind considers your ideal ride as always true!

1. **Think of a belief you know is true.**

   Think of something you know is absolutely true all of the time. Think about something you know in your heart of hearts. The sun coming up tomorrow? Night follows day? Breathing keeps us alive? Do you have a picture for this belief?

   a) Notice now the location of the picture, i.e., think of the picture on a screen in your minds eye. Is it straight in front of you? To the left or right? Up a bit or down a bit? Place your hand where it comes from.
   b) Write down where it is located on your mental screen, in the box below.
   c) Now notice whether you are watching yourself in the picture. Note that down.
   d) We will call this your 'strong belief' picture.
   e) Clear your mental screen. Look around the room, take some refreshing breaths.

   > Strong, absolute belief
   >
   > Location of picture:
   >
   > Are you watching yourself in the picture? (Yes or no)

2. **Think of something that is no longer true for you.**

   You're no longer 16? 21?

   You're no longer at school?

   Example: "I am 16."

Notice first of all the language, "I am 16." (**No longer true.**)

Compare that with

- "I am no longer 16." (True.)
- "I was 16." (Also true; we need a statement that is **no longer true**.)

Now, when you think about that statement (I am 16):

a) Do you have a picture? Again, notice where that is on your mental screen: centre, left, right, up or down.
b) Where is the picture located on the screen in your mind? Place your hand there.
c) Make a note of the location in the box below.
d) Are you watching yourself in the picture? Note that too.
e) We will call this your 'no longer true' picture.
f) Clear your mental screen. Look around the room, take some refreshing breaths.

No longer true

Location of picture:

Are you watching yourself in the picture? (Yes or no)

You now have a strong, absolute belief and a no longer true picture.

3. What issues are you having with your riding?

a) Do you have a picture? Where is it located on your mental screen? Place your hand there.
b) Move the 'riding issue' picture's location and your hand to the same place as the 'no longer true' picture.
c) If there is a difference in whether you are watching yourself or not for 'riding issue' and 'no longer true' make the 'riding issue' have the same as 'no longer true'
d) Now make the picture smaller and darker, shrinking it down to less than a speck of dust.
e) If there were any sounds with this 'riding issue' picture, including your own internal chatter, turn them down and put them on mute.

4. What compelling, successful and attractive image of you riding do you want now?

a) Do you have a picture? Make sure it's a 'wow' picture, perfectly positive!
b) Where is it located on the screen in your mind? Place your hand in that position.
c) Move that picture and your hand into the location of the 'strong belief' picture in your mind.
d) Make sure you see that picture as you did the 'strong belief' one, watching yourself or not.

e) Now let's hype up your picture. Make it big if that makes it more compelling
f) Turn up the brightness and colours if that makes it more compelling
g) What sounds are important? Voices in your head? Footfall of your horse? Turn them up to the most compelling. Add music if you want to.
h) Think about the tone of the sounds. Often deeper sounds are more intense and help to seal in the new belief.
i) Have that picture as big, bold, bright and loud so as to make it the most fantastic image you can imagine.
j) Seal in that picture by imagining it being sealed in a sandwich box. Hear the lid click onto the tub.
k) Clear your mental screen. Look around the room, take some refreshing breaths.

5. Check your beliefs

a) Ask yourself: now how do I feel about my riding issues?
b) Ask yourself: when I next go to do X, how do I feel about actually doing it?

6. When you go to ride or compete

a) Bring your image up onto your screen. Big, bold, bright and loud. Make it grow bigger in front of you. Clear the screen.
b) Repeat at least 5 times.

All horses are blue: a note on general affirmations

For most people, saying general affirmations cannot change beliefs. If I told you to repeat, "I'm a calm confident rider at all times," it may help very little or not at all. The reason is that such generalised affirmations are good at changing your mood or state, but not in changing an unconsciously held belief. Your unconscious mind will reject anything that goes against your deeply set beliefs. For example, I want you to believe that all horses are blue. I know that you think they are black, white, grey, chestnut, beige and brown: actually they are blue. Say, "All horses are blue." Keep saying it. This will feel very silly and totally false. Your mind will reject it and keep reminding you of all the non-blue horses! Now, let me show you a grey horse that has been covered from head to hoof in blue chalk. Then you would tell me that, yes, that one was blue, but underneath it's grey. You can't change your beliefs simply by affirmation statements. The new way of thinking has to have come from your own experience, something that sounds and feels right for you. New beliefs have to be part of your model of the world, part of your reality, to really work.

R,R&R Chapter 4

Now, give yourself a well-earned break, there's a lot of work in Chapter 4. Celebrate your victories. Stop for a few days of **reflection, rest and relaxation.** Practise the techniques; you can get someone to read out the instructions for you or even record them you're your phone. Pause here until you feel that there is no pressure to start Chapter 5. Here is a quick summary of Chapter 4.

- We can shift our perception of limiting ideas and beliefs by practising a variety of techniques including:
    - Using a meaning reframe
    - Using a context reframe
    - Questioning your limiting belief
    - Using the 'Changing a limiting belief using a 4-way visualisation'.

- New beliefs have to be part of your model of the world, part of your reality, to really work, that's why affirmations are usually limited in their success.

Chapter 4 - What did you learn? How will you use this to boost your riding confidence?

5. Breaking down the problem even more!

When problems or issues arise, we categorise them, analyse them and describe them using our language. We can state what the problem is and how bad it feels for us. We may be able to specify when the issues began and even add more detail as time goes by. All this is done using words: speaking to others and using our own inner self-talk.

We can demonstrate this idea using the diagram below:

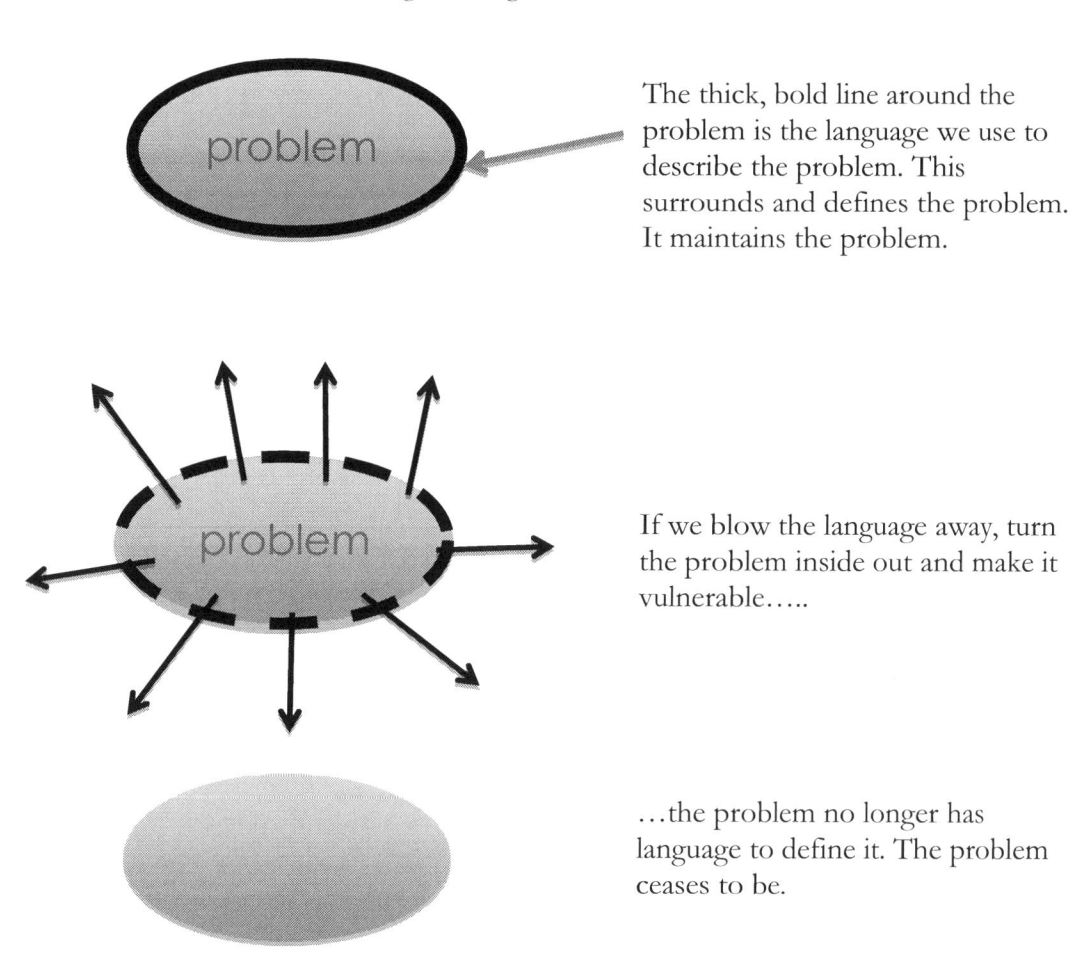

The thick, bold line around the problem is the language we use to describe the problem. This surrounds and defines the problem. It maintains the problem.

If we blow the language away, turn the problem inside out and make it vulnerable…..

…the problem no longer has language to define it. The problem ceases to be.

☐ **Task:** To begin the process, we use question sets that work at the unconscious level. These are called Quantum Linguistics and, as the name suggests cause leaps of understanding in the unconscious mind.

We want to start to break your old problem down now. We're going to have your mind work on a few questions. All you have to do is relax, go with the flow of the questions and let the most automatic answers pop into your head.

The questions will sound a little unusual; try not to analyse or over-think the questions, *try not to make sense of them*. Don't worry if you're confused by the wording; that's a really good sign! Just let the most automatic answer come out, it doesn't matter if it makes no sense. There are no right or wrong answers, this is just getting to the crux of the matter in your mind.

Read the question, pause and move onto the next. Give a verbal answer only when asked.

Going beyond the boundaries of the problem – give automatic verbal answers

- What is your problem?
- What is your problem not?
- How do you know what the problem is not?
- What is it that you need to not know to know this?

Decision destroyer

- Think about your problem now, think about when you first started to feel that way. We could say 'when' you decided to feel that way…..do you have a picture?
- Where were you when you decided to feel this way?
- Just before you made that decision, where were you?
- Thinking about that time, freeze frame. Notice that you had many options on how to react. A full spectrum of outcomes: from very positive to very negative and all the shades of outcomes inbetween. Can you notice all those alternative paths now?
- NOW, as you think about your present situation, notice how many options you have…to do things differently now

- Think of that problem and notice how you feel now
- As you think about the next time you XX, knowing what you know now, notice how much better you feel, not doing it
-
-

Time scramble

- What would it be like when you have made those changes now?
- Go inside your mind and try in vain to have the same problem
- As you think about it now, if you could make this change for yourself so that you could STOP…having made that change and see yourself now riding with full confidence right now. Do you like the way you look if you could make that change and look back and see yourself having made that change now!

☐ **Task:** Now ask yourself: what's the problem?! (Try in vain to put it into words.)

If you had to think for a second, it means that you had trouble accessing the correct language to define the problem and the problem is already breaking down. If you could recall the problem without thinking, go over the questions, then wait a day or two for the questions to permeate your unconscious mind and for you to know it consciously.

R,R&R Chapter 5

Now for a few days of **reflection, rest and relaxation.** We've loosened up and broken down the boundaries of your riding issues using a lot of Quantum Linguistics, so there is no rush to get onto Chapter 6. Slow down, repeat the question sets and enjoy all the ways in which you're changing! Here is a quick summary of Chapter 5.

- We define a problem using our language. When the problem is beginning to break down, we often experience this as an inability to describe the problem in words easily.
- We can use Quantum Linguistics question sets to tunnel deep into the unconscious mind to provoke the change we want to make.

Chapter 5 - What did you learn? How will you use this to boost your riding confidence?

6. Diminishing and dissolving fears

If you're reading this course continuously, i.e., at a steady pace with no long breaks between chapters, then you're really ready to dissolve any lingering fears: right now! If you've taken a break from the course and just returned, read the previous chapters again and read through your notes. This will act as a reminder of all the work you've already accumulated and establish the correct frame of mind to continue successfully.

Introduction

Fear manifests in a variety of behaviours and is as individual as you are. For some, it means withdrawing and become quiet, alone with our thoughts, whilst others will chatter and have a great desire to talk about everything and anything! Notice what your behaviours are. Do you feel butterflies, become nauseous; do your hands shake and your legs weaken? Maybe you lose the ability to focus on anything other than the fear and dread.

It may come as a surprise that there are only two innate fears: heights and loud noises. All other fears have been learnt, directly or indirectly. The good news is that our responses to a particular situation can be re-learnt and re-crafted (think about how much of your school work you've unlearnt!). What's more, fear can be eliminated far more quickly than you may imagine. Several equestrian articles reiterate that confidence requires a long time to build, whereas a set-back can remove confidence instantly. Yes, but only if we let it. Only if we allow ourselves to install the fear into our minds and run the 'fear programme'. Only if we don't counter the 'fear programme' with a more compelling alternative. That's what this book is all about: finding a way to learn from mistakes, move on and remain confident in our ability.

Riders often define their anxieties in terms of specific times, a life-event or change of horse. For example, many people will tell their coach their age and explain that they've always been a nervous rider. Some will describe their fear as being part of parenthood and the need to be safe for their children. Others will have noticed their nerves increasing after an accident or in acquiring a horse with new quirks or they will simply put it down to getting older! These explanations are often a means of describing how ingrained their fears are. The reason for mentioning this is absolutely not to belittle those fears (they are very real to us!), but to convey gently that the fear can be removed; not a one of us is a lost cause!

How fear arises

Simply put, we condition ourselves to fear something. We may not exert any conscious effort in establishing a fear. Unfortunately, unconsciously, we have built it up with a degree of success! Over time, we have added colour to our images, scary sounds and run the full gamut of negative, highly charged emotions. We have attached certain visual or auditory triggers too, to make us feel nervous at the very thought of facing our fear, before we're even on board. Subjective experiences are transformed into emotional experiences.

We've done this so often, we have created a habit, one that we can repeat automatically! Additionally, we've analysed our present situation, over and over and our inner voice can call up any tag line sure to make us feel worse. Our fears may grow. The jumps that were easy become 3 feet bigger, the competition that was a fun, schooling exercise becomes a do-or-die state of affairs, cantering is done at 100 mph and hacking is equivalent to crossing a 6-laned motorway. The fears are looming larger, becoming even more heightened. How do other's opinions affect you? How has talking about your fears affected your riding in the past? Have your fears worsened, lessened or stayed the same? Notice whether you feel comfortable being watched or having others present. At this juncture, we have two choices: we can either procrastinate and give up, or find a way to enjoy confident, harmonious riding now. You are reading this, because you have chosen the latter; understanding how your mind conjures up the fear can have a real benefit in deciding how to undo it. Importantly, by recognising how fears are generated, we can stop ourselves feeding current fears and germinating news ones.

☐ **Task:** Which comes first, the fear or the symptoms of fear?

Consider the following:

1. A conscious thought or learning has been amplified to represent a fear.
2. The fear is reinforced until it is a habit, it's automatic and unconscious.
3. An unconscious, involuntary thought (i.e., one we are not aware of) can lead to the physiological symptoms of fear and *only then* do we become conscious of the fact that we are frightened. In other words, we have the symptoms of fear (feeling nauseous, dry mouth, sweaty palms, jelly legs etc.), ever so slightly *before* we realise we're frightened. How can this make sense?!
4. The cycle quickens each time we have the same initial unconscious thought.
5. Fear becomes automatic in that situation.
6. Conscious need to break this unconscious cycle.

Once the fear becomes unconscious and habitual, the symptoms follow, even if there is no reason to fear. For example, have you ever become anxious when someone else was about to do the thing that unnerves you the most? Look out for these signs. It's a clue that your fear may be 'inappropriate'. For example, I used to groom for friends when they competed and I was more nervous than them!

Appropriate versus inappropriate fears

Consciously recognising whether a fear is appropriate or not is another impactful means of starting to dissolve the inappropriate ones.

Task: List your fears in a table like the one below. Let's call your fear 'your old fear', after all, it's in the past now. Be specific. Tick the column 'inappropriate' (a perceived, larger-than-life fear) or 'appropriate' (a real fear, true peril and danger). Choose the column without thinking, choose quickly. This makes the task more for your unconscious mind, than your logical conscious mind. Then read on, to find out how we can compare and identify each type of fear.

My old fear	Is this fear appropriate?	Is this fear inappropriate?

As discussed in Chapter 2, the unconscious mind is our ultimate protector. It functions to protect us from real and perceived threats in much the same manner. A real threat, a threat to our safety happens in the moment, the split second where we unconsciously act to save ourselves from true danger. This is not a threat we have to think about or analyse, we don't need to feel continuously anxious for the protective set of actions to engage. This type of fear serves us, it saves us from high level danger. Is it far more rare in reality that we have convinced ourselves? That depends on your activity; riding is certainly not risk-free. However, in that sudden moment when your horse bolts, rears, spins or bucks, what saves you? Your analytical mind, weighing up the situation, deciding what to do, deducing the pros and cons, or the reflexive action of your unconscious mind? Which part of the mind are you putting your faith in? Your unconscious mind is there for you whenever and wherever you need it. Always. You don't have to niggle away at it to remind it that there is a danger! You can relax! Always!

Perceived, inappropriate fears ensue as a result of focusing on what we don't want, rather than the more attractive focusing on what we do. The amalgamation of sights, sounds, negative feelings, even an intensified certainty in the importance of what others think can lead to an involuntary, deep belief that a particular threat is real. Inappropriate fears announce themselves when there is actually nothing happening. They are present when there is no real danger. How many times have you felt sick to your stomach before even getting on your horse? This type of fear is often blown out of proportion and this is the fear that hinders us. We're mentally held back by the all-consuming negative thoughts flooding our conscious minds, we lack concentration (apart from paying great attention to the negative 'what ifs') and we lack focus. We focus on the other horses in the collecting ring, we focus on jump number 3, not what we're currently jumping, we focus on horses in a neighbouring field or we walk around the arena thinking about uncontrollable speed. In conjunction with mental blocks, we are physically stifled. Our aids are not clear, we position our hands and legs exactly where we have been trained not to! The strength in our legs diminishes, but our hands may become too strong. We don't use our core muscles correctly and our shoulders rise up to our chins. Consequently, we ride less well that we know we can; our performance decreases.

Naturally, we can have a combination of appropriate and inappropriate fears. This is quite a hazardous condition. This would be the over-horsed rider, or someone riding at a much higher level than they have trained for.

Reconsider your fears now. How do you feel about your fears? How do you feel knowing that an inappropriate fear is causing you to be mentally and physically blocked and that dissolving that fear will not lessen your ridden responses, not prevent you reacting when necessary, but enable you to be a more sensitive, attentive rider?

☐ Task:

1. When next feeling anxious practise being aware of fear striking.

2. Practise knowing the triggers. See Chapter 8 for the peripheral vision technique 'Hakalau' to help you to step back and recover your composure.

3. Take a breath: what are the **real** dangers? What is perceived, imagined and over-anticipated?

4. Write down 'Real fear? Now relax' on a piece of paper, as you write 'Now relax,' feel a soothing wave of relaxation coursing through your body. Imagine it, feel it, enjoy it. Really emphasise that lovely deeply relaxing feeling. Put the paper in your pocket. You may not be able to pull it out as you ride, you may be able to touch your pocket or even just know it's there as a reminder. See the words in your mind's eye, see your writing as you ride. Remember the words; remember the soothing feeling of being relaxed.

5. As you ride, get a friend or instructor to ask you, or even ask yourself, "What am I focusing on?"

"Are my shoulders/arms/hands/core muscles/buttocks/legs/feet too tense?"

Practise asking yourself these questions until it becomes second nature to re-align your thoughts and muscles to what you are doing.

6. When riding, ride from moment to moment, second to second, rather than imagining a future disaster.

7. Skip ahead to Chapter 8 for techniques to practise whilst riding

Did you do the exercises above? If you did, wonderful, which helped the most? How will you personalise the technique? If you didn't do the exercises, are you afraid they will work, or that they won't? Are you open-minded enough to try? Only by practising the techniques will you find the perfect one for your unconscious mind! Alternatively if you didn't complete the task because your fear is paralysing you, try the above at home, imagining riding and completing the task successfully several times. Now find a quiet space at the stables to do the same. Then ask a friend to be with you when you try on horseback for the first time.

Adrenaline, fear and excitement

When we first encounter something new, our bodies often produce adrenaline. That gives us a feeling of anticipation. In some, especially in children, that will create the physiology of excitement; in others, it will register as fear. In NLP, we are said to create our idea of reality based on the all the sensory input into our brains – everything we see, hear, feel touch, taste and smell, is made sense of, by constructing our view of the world. Two people in the same situation can experience that event in different ways. How often have you recounted a memorable event with someone else who was there, only to find that their recollection is different to your own? (Think about how we filter reality, see Chapter 1.) This is the same dichotomy observed in those that interpret the adrenaline as fear and those who consider it excitement.

As adults, we learn to feel uncomfortable in new situations. We learn to dislike that adrenaline. We reason with ourselves that we don't like this feeling. Now, in essence, we fear more and become excited less. When the flight or fight response of adrenaline is initiated, it translates into making us feel scared. Scared of feeling excited.

Gaining a clearer understanding of the mechanisms of fear allow us to identify courage more easily. Courage is the person who used to feel fear being able to control their state now, knowing that they are responsible for how they feel.

The three common riding fears and how to overcome them

The three common fears are:

- Falling off
- Loss of control
- Failure – feeling/looking less of a rider than you really are

Remember, a good instructor will work wonders to help you through the practicalities of good riding techniques, lessons or training sessions will work hand in hand with the exercises for the mind outlined here.

Falling off

Most people who ride fall off! At one time or another, even great riders part company with their horse. Make sure you always ride in a suitable hat and possibly a body protector. For those who complain that body protectors are bulky and uncomfortable, there are lightweight ones to choose from now; if it eliminates the fear of hurting yourself if you fall off, gives you confidence, then that's reason enough to wear one. Never mind what others think or how you will look! Prioritise what is important to you.

If the mere thought of falling off is paralysing to you, then you will ride so rigidly that you may not be able to absorb the change in direction of a shying horse or the run-out at a fence. It becomes a self-fulfilling prophesy: you get what you focus on. Focusing on falling off, often leads to us falling off.

Remember too that core stability and spinal alignment have a lot to do with feeling secure in a saddle. Exercise programmes such as Pilates (or EquiPilates™) can help with your physical approach.

Loss of control

Think about riding one stride. That's it for now. Visualise riding one stride. Visualise the perfect stride for the gait and consider where your centre of gravity is, where are the horses legs and what are your hands and legs doing? Repeat!

Now visualise each section of your ride individually, think in small steps, see your successful completion. Visualise your view from the horse, hear the steady footfall, know that you are moving with the horse. Take yourself very slowly and steadily through the ride: in slow-motion. See the different sights, keeping your eyes parallel with the ground. All the time, moving very slowly and staying fully in control. Notice how you change your balance as you ride curves and corners. Notice how good it feels to ride in synergy with the horse. Are your muscles tight? Relax your muscles, drop your shoulders. Repeat at least 5 times just before mounting. Continue to think about your ride in slow-motion, thinking about letting go of muscle tensions as you ride.

Failure

Failure emanates from a lack of self-belief. See Chapter 4 for advice on removing a limiting belief. Visualise your ride, as in the 'loss of control' paragraph above. If doubtful self-talk plagues you, turn the volume dial down, until you can't make out the words or intent of the voice. Do the same if you suffer from what others may think, turn their voices down, then off. You may wish to drown out criticism using your favourite up-beat music. If you dislike people watching you ride, see the colour drain out of them, turn them black and white and allow them to fade away into the far distance.

R,R&R Chapter 6

Reflection, rest and relaxation. Just what you need right now to consolidate all that change work! Here's a quick summary of Chapter 6.

- There are only two innate fears: heights and loud noises. All other fears have been learnt, directly or indirectly. Anything that is learnt can be unlearnt.
- Once the fear becomes unconscious and habitual, the symptoms follow, even if there is no reason to fear.

- Consciously recognising whether a fear is appropriate or not is another impactful means of starting to dissolve the inappropriate ones.
- Fears ensue as a result of focusing on what we don't want, rather than the more attractive focusing on what we do
- Focus on what you want – this is a powerful, clear instruction to your unconscious mind

Chapter 6 - What did you learn? How will you use this to boost your riding confidence?

7. More advanced mind techniques

1. Give your unconscious mind something else to consider:

This is a good technique for those who have what ifs running through their mind

- As you think through your fear, do you have a picture? A movie?
- At home, view the picture or play the movie, change the colour to black and white.
- Step out of the picture, so you are watching yourself in the picture.
- Make the picture small, dark, gloomy; shrink it down to the upper left hand corner
- Shrink it so that it becomes a dot, then disappears
- Notice that you feel as though you've sent it away
- Repeat several times; now practice this just before getting on
- As you ride, anytime the picture or movie enters your head, go through the steps to push it out of your mind
- Practise this until the gloomy picture requires effort to recover – warning – don't expend any effort trying to recover the gloomy picture, let it go, let it disappear.
- Not working? Did you try to maintain that gloomy picture? Allow it to disappear
- Compose a perfectly attractive picture where everything goes well. Adjust the colour to be just as you want it, then do the same for sounds. Turn down any unhelpful internal dialogue. Are there any smells you would like to add in, just to make the image even more compelling? Add in the feelings you want. As you think of the picture, with all the wonderful sights and sounds, really *feel the emotions* linked to it. Turn up your dial for those great feelings, turn them up further. Make sure you're in the picture and not watching yourself. Seal that picture in. Now, go through the bullets steps above, again. After your gloomy picture has disappeared, blow the compelling picture onto the screen. See it as a huge, glorious technicolour picture in front of you. Continue to switch between pictures until the gloomy one no longer exists.

2. Anchors away! A technique called 'Collapse Anchors' to remove generalised or specific fear

Removing an unhelpful negative feeling or association (anchor). This involves imagining a scenario whilst pressing a knuckle. This is said to 'anchor' that feeling to the knuckle. The timing needs to be good, so that this has maximum effect.

1. When you think of your current situation, do you have a picture? This 'negative' current issue anchored to the first knuckle, by picturing your current situation, then pressing index finger onto the knuckle as soon as you **start** to feel the emotion, remove finger as the emotion **just begins** to subside.

2. Think of a set of 5-6 positive emotions you want to feel when you ride e.g., successful, confident, relaxed, motivated, in harmony, happy. Take it one emotion at a time. For each one, decide on a time when you felt that emotion strongly. Do you have a picture? As the feeling **starts**, touch the second knuckle, as soon as the feelings **begin** to decline, remove finger from knuckle. Repeat for all your positive emotions, stacking the anchors on top of each other on your second knuckle.

3. Press first and second knuckle together for at least 20 seconds.

4. Remove the finger touching the 'negative' anchor – first knuckle - and keep pressing positive anchors for about 5 more seconds

3. Removing fear from a specific negative memory

e.g., previous injury or bad experience – simplified Fast Phobia Method.

1. Set yourself up a 'resource anchor' (See Chapter 8 for more details or follow Step 2 of the above). That is a way to recall strong, positive feelings. Now when you press your knuckle, you will feel those positive feelings again. Throughout the rest of this technique, you can touch your knuckle for 5-15 seconds to evoke those feelings if you need to at ay time during the rest of this exercise.

2. Score yourself 0-10 for how bad the fear is, 0 being a non-entity, 10 being really terrible.

3. When you think about your fear, do you have a picture? Make a short 5-10 second movie of the problem, with the first and last frames being positions of calm, safety and positivity.

4. Close your eyes. Run the movie for 5-10 seconds. Remember the first frame of the moving is a position of complete calm and safety, as is the last frame.

5. In a moment, you will alternate running the movie backwards and forwards.

6. Put the first frame of the movie up on the screen, watch yourself in the movie, in black and white, run the movie forwards at normal speed, go!

7. Last frame of the movie up on the screen, you're acting in the movie now, make it colour. Run it backwards at normal speed, go!

8. Put the first frame of the movie up on the screen, watch yourself in the movie, in black and white, run the movie forwards at normal speed, go!

9. From now on, alternate going backwards and then forwards. In the backwards part, go faster with each round: 2x normal speed, 5x normal speed, 10x normal speed, 20x normal speed, 30x normal speed, 50x normal speed, 100x normal speed.

10. Ask yourself how do you feel about that old fear now, score yourself 0-10 for how bad the old fear is, 0 being a non-entity, 10 being really terrible. Repeat until score is 0. This may take several repeats, but rest assured the old movie will fade or disappear or fragment and with it, will go the fear.

4. Using a language pattern – questioning the fear using more quantum linguistics

Read these questions to yourself, do not analyse their meaning, do not seek to find the 'correct' answer (there isn't one!). Ask yourself each question and pause – do you have an inner-voice answer, a feeling, a thought or picture? The answers may not be direct and the results may take time for your unconscious mind to have worked on. Persevere with your insights!

Language set 1

- What's the problem?
- How do you know it's a problem?
- When did you decide that?
- When don't you do the problem now?
- What are you not deciding when you don't do it?
- How is it different from how you were?
- How do you know that, now?
- What other changes would you like to make?

Language set 2

- Say the issue/problem out loud
- Say more (until you have said <u>everything</u> you can think of)
- What is it that you haven't said that you're NOT thinking of right now? *click of fingers* **Now answer immediately**
- Consider that old problem now, *click of fingers* how is it different now? **Answer immediately**

5. Using the Anxiety Model

This is my version of the Anxiety Model and is based on the premise that anxiety is a fear of something that is in the future. This is a powerful technique to remind the unconscious mind that the future is not happening at this moment.

1. Consider the ride or competition you are worried about.
2. Picture yourself 15 minutes *after* the 100% *successful completion* of this ride
3. Imagine what you are seeing, hearing and feeling. You must imagine it to be 100% successful for this method to work
4. Repeat 3-5 times
5. Now, how do you feel about that ride?

What if it doesn't work? This method works when you imagine 100% success and 100% completion. If the anxiety isn't alleviated, you may have had doubts, you may not have imagined 100% success or full completion of your ride.

A note about secondary gain

Sometimes, when we've been burdened with an issue for long period, either the issue begins to define who we are or it acts as a safety barrier, giving us an excuse not to eliminate our fears. This is known as 'secondary gain'. The unconscious mind gains more from holding onto the fear than letting it go. You may encounter the rider with secondary gain who tries to denigrate your efforts to overcome your fears. This is usually because they gain something by maintaining their own fears.

Secondary gainers sometimes use their fear to seek attention from others, they are proud of their status and wear it like a badge of honour. Nobody could ever help them to remove their fears, because their fears are so ingrained/much worse than everyone else's/based on worse experiences than everyone else. Beware of the secondary gain rider! They will not be 'at cause', but will show classic signs of being 'at effect'. They will blame others and their horse and, worse, they will drain you of your own energy and resolve. They could even plant sufficient seeds of doubt in your unconscious mind so that you buy into their views and insecurities.

Be prepared to continue to loosen and remove your fears quietly and without fuss, ignoring their negativity. You may know someone who hides behind a fear, this person doesn't truly want to be less afraid – but they will give you all the advice you want (and plenty that you don't) to remove *your* issues. So, I'll say it now, beware!! They will mock your efforts (and cover up their jealousy).

"Don't take away all my fear"

I hear this all the time. The alternative is, "I need a bit of fear/nerves to make me sharp/make me concentrate." This is a myth. If you have nerves, your fight or flight response has kicked in rapidly already. The pre-frontal cortex of your brain, responsible for planning, reasoning, decision-making, focus and inhibiting counterproductive impulses is much slower. It's not that the pre-frontal cortex is inhibited, but that it's outpaced. Use your prefrontal cortex now: decide whether you want the nervous edge that riders speak of and you want it to overshadow those higher functions.

R,R&R Chapter 7

Reflection, rest and relaxation time again. Take several days to get to grips with these techniques. Consider which ones you can use before you ride or the night before you ride. Here's a quick summary of Chapter 7.

- Different techniques will have differing levels of success, depending on how yur unconscious mind works.
- Visualisations, confusion techniques (including the modified Fast Phobia Model), anchoring, quantum linguistics and the Anxiety Model will work for different people on different issues and at different times. Find out which methods you prefer to practise.
- Secondary gain is when the unconscious mind gains more from holding onto the fear than letting it go. Beware the secondary gainers who may make you doubt your efforts.
- Riders who want to have a bit of fear because they see it as a means of having an alertness or edge are actually scuppering their own performance by overshadowing higher functions of the brain such as planning, reasoning, decision-making, focus and inhibiting counterproductive impulses.

Chapter 7 - What did you learn? How will you use this to boost your riding confidence?

8. What to do whilst riding - building confidence whilst in the saddle

I can remember travelling to competitions and merrily chatting away, having forgotten my fears momentarily. Then I'd remember that I was supposed to be nervous. My mind would compensate for this 'wasted' time and make me feel even worse! If only I'd known about 'state control'! This means that you have it in your power the ability to control your emotional state. This is not magic or unachievable, it's what everybody's unconscious mind can do for them. It's only when left unattended, that the unconscious mind chooses an unresourceful emotional state, usually to do with a habit it has formed.

I want to give you a set of techniques to control your state that can be done in the saddle – after all, no matter how hard you work on your mind skills, the proof of the pudding is actually how you feel whilst on board.

1. Resource anchor

An anchor is set when we have an intense feeling or experience and at the same time, we see, hear, touch, smell or taste something; the two experiences become neurologically linked. The anchor can be fired off when we next see, hear, touch, smell or taste the same thing. An example would be hearing a favourite piece of music that takes us back to a special memory; seeing a photo that brings back fond feelings or even smelling haylage! We make our own anchors. How would it be to call upon powerful resourceful feelings right on cue? If we link the powerful feelings to a sight or touch, then when we see or touch the next time, we'll recall the feelings we need.

1. Think of 6 feelings you want to have whilst riding, here are some common examples, although you may want to use your own:

    - Confidence
    - Enthusiasm
    - Determination
    - Motivation
    - Happiness
    - Calm
    - Successful
    - Being in harmony with your horse
    - Inner knowledge of your skills

2. Choose your preferred anchor type:

- For a **visual anchor** – this can be the sight of your horse's neck or, one I use with clients, have a small sticky spot, the type from stationers, stuck on the back of the bridle. Take one feeling from your list at a time. Recall a time when you felt this intensely. As you go back to that time, float down into your body, see what you saw, hear what you heard and really feel that feeling. As soon as you have hint of that feeling coming back to you, look at your horse's neck/sticky dot. As the emotion begins to decline, look away. Repeat for 4-5 other feelings, looking at the same anchor.
- For a **touch (kinaesthetic) anchor** – this can be touching your first knuckle or touching your horse's wither. Take one feeling from your list at a time. Recall a time when you felt this intensely. As you go back to that time, float down into your body, see what you saw, hear what you heard and really feel that feeling. As soon as a you have hint of that feeling coming back to you, press firmly onto your first knuckle or horse's withers, then remove the touch as the emotion begins to decline.

3. To test: look at your visual cue or touch your kinaesthetic cue for about 20-30 seconds. How do you feel? Add more feelings onto your anchor if it is not intense enough for you to feel good.

4. Refresh your anchor as needed. The anchor may weaken over time, as we may look at the visual cue or touch the kinaesthetic one whilst not feeling so good or even feeling neutral.

2. Hakalau

This is a technique from Ancient Hawaii! It is sometimes called soft-eye or using peripheral vision. This process can be used for any riding issues. The key is your ability to get in touch with the whole problem. The technique works by hi-lighting and removing the boundary (language) of the problem dissolving it.

Going into Hakalau – practise unmounted, then on your horse:

- "Pick a spot on the wall. As you focus on it, now pay attention to the peripheral part of your vision." Click fingers.
- Pick a spot above your eye line in front of you. Keep focussing on that spot, taking in all the colours, textures, light/shadow and really focussing in.
- Keep going for about 20 seconds.

- Now allow your vision to extend slightly, so that you are looking at the spot and about 30cm either side, slowly take your vision out a little more and more until you can't focus on the spot, but you can see your hands if you stretch your arms out level with your shoulders.

- Now stretch your vision even wider. Even wider! Now you're in peripheral vision.

- If you start to think about your issues, you will probably drop out of peripheral vision, as you focus on the negative thoughts and feelings. This is due to there being a really useful wiring of our brains: you cannot be in Hakalau (peripheral vision) and have a negative thought at the same time. It's a mutually exclusive thing! Practise remaining in Hakalau as you go about your daily life, so that you can easily switch to peripheral vision whilst riding.

- Great for dressage – you have a better awareness of the letters around the arena and your transitions become crisper

- Great for show-jumping and cross country – you are far more alert to where the next jump is and the jump after that, so your striding and ability to line the horse up improves

- Great for hacking – you are aware of the obstacles around you, the pheasants in the hedge, the cyclist up ahead, the plastic bag blowing your way

3. Breathing technique

Sometimes you need something to take your mind off your riding! This is a very easy way to occupy the conscious mind and prevent it from being the devil on your shoulder. Choose your gait – walk, trot, canter and be very aware of your horse's footfalls.

Now breathe in for 4 footfalls, out for 4 footfalls
Now breathe in for 5 footfalls, out for 5 footfalls
Now breathe in for 6 footfalls, out for 6 footfalls

You can also use the 3,4,5 method. Simply inhale for 3 seconds, hold for 4 seconds and exhale for 5 seconds. And repeat….

4. Visualisation from Chapter 4

Use the 'Belief change' we covered in Chapter 4 and see your new, compelling picture blown up big, bright and loud in front of you. Make it grown bigger, louder. Repeat x5

5. Mindfulness

Mindfulness requires you to live in the moment. In so doing, you quiet the mind to any thinking about events that have happened in the past or events that may or may not happen in the future. You are totally absorbed in the current moment, that millisecond, that 'point of power' as Louise Hay described it. Because, that is the only moment you can ever change. By becoming focussed entirely in the present, this heightens your awareness and alertness: a compelling state for any rider to be in. Enjoy the stillness you find in that single moment by using one or more of these mindfulness methods.

- Think about each ridden stride at walk. Consider the single stride. How can you make that single stride the best and most advantageous for the movement you want the horse to perform? Think about that one stride, where is your weight, your centre of gravity, your hands, your legs and feet? Make that stride the best that it can be. With more practise, you'll be able to quicken up and achieve results in different gaits, speeds, impulsions, bends and circles

- Sit in halt and scan your body in walk. Consider where your balance is, move down your body sequentially; think about whether each body part needs to move forwards or back, up or down to achieve the position you want; consider adjusting your head, neck, shoulder tops, shoulder blades, collar bones, ribcage, waist on each side, hips, seat bones, hands, fingers, thumbs, forearms, elbows, thighs, lower legs, ankles, feet. As you scan adjust for a good riding position, breathe into that body part (imagine the breath entering it and then coming back via your lungs to be exhaled) and release the tension. Think – position – breathe – release

- This can be practiced in any gait and is really good for collection and extension work. Think about the stride you want, collected or extended. Have inside your head the footfall tempo. Now, breathe in for 4 strides, out for 4 strides, repeat until you are happy that you control the speed and impulsion level. Change between collected and extended, breathe in for 4, out for 4, but notice how your breathing has changed. Now what about breathing in for 6 out for 6? Change the footfall counts to keep your mind occupied and change your collection and extension to keep your horse on their toes too (figuratively speaking!). This is super for anyone who has a horse that is likely to bolt – by practising this exercise in an arena, you can feel the control you have to ride in a more open space.

- Talk to your unconscious mind! Give your mind a pat on the back and a convincing mantra to listen to. Again, this keeps you in the moment. I like to use, "I'm alright now…..and now……and now……and now," timed with my breathing. It has a hypnotic style that calms you down and communicates to your unconscious mind that you're fine in that moment. Once you string several moments together, your unconscious mind relaxes into a new habit.

- If your horse will stand in halt, you can also try this one. Clear your mind. You're only going to sit in halt, no further on in your riding. Hold one hand over the withers, with the lightest of touches about 1-3mm away from your horse's withers, so you can just feel the tips of the hairs. Breathe deeply. Keep watching your horse, this can take time. You're waiting for a slower blink than normal from them. Maybe a loosening of the lower lip, a snort, a changing breathing or even a yawn. Focus on having no tension in your hand and focus on your horse's physiology. And wait. If there's no response, lighten the touch or press slightly less lightly. Play with what your horse 'hears'. You can also try the poll if you can reach or feel OK to sit forward and repeat in the same way. Now that you've entered your horse's world, allow time to slow down. Give yourself several minutes to do this, it will feel like forever and your human mind will want to get on with the riding. Resist the temptation to rush; instead go with the flow, breathe, communicate with the horse, have that relaxing conversation and enjoy. This lightness of touch can be relaxing for you and for your horse. The channels of communication between you are opened.

- Try a free mindfulness recording, go to https://www.traceycolenlp.com/meditation-mindfulness-hypnosis/, click play and relax.

R,R&R Chapter 8

This chapter can be read chronologically or stand-alone. Whenever you read it, it's good to still keep to your **reflection, rest and relaxation.** Choose the techniques that work for you and are quick and easy to remember. It's also good to give your mind some praise for all it's doing for you. It's changing your neurology, so tell it how great it's doing, it really works on positive reinforcement! Here's a quick summary of Chapter 8.

- If you are a kinaesthic person (you like learning by doing, you're practical), you may like
    - Resource anchors (touch anchors), the breathing techniques, Hakalau, the mindfulness example where you touch your horse's withers or poll in halt.
    - Pat yourself on the back to let your mind know that you appreciate what it's doing.

- If you are an auditory person or you chat away inside your own head a lot, you may like
    - To talk yourself through any of the techniques, hear the instructions as you do them; in particular, you may like to repeat the mindfulness, "I'm alright now and now and now…."
    - Tell yourself that you're doing well to let your mind know that you appreciate what it's doing.
- If you are a visual person, you may like
    - Resource (visual) anchor, any visualisations, Hakalau
    - See yourself riding the way that you want to and smile to let your mind know that you appreciate what it's doing.

Chapter 8 - What did you learn? How will you use this to boost your riding confidence?

9. FAQs and closing comments

FAQs

1. **Can I do these techniques on other people?**

   No, unless you are a certified Practitioner of NLP, these techniques are for your personal use only

2. **I'm not a very visual person, which techniques would work best for me?**

   None of the techniques require that you have a photographic quality to the visualisations; the mind's eye image can be built on sights, sounds and feelings too. However, Collapse Anchors in Chapter 5 requires more feelings than sights and might be good for you to try.

3. **How long do these techniques last? Can the confidence wear off?**

   By breaking a habit and forming a new, more compelling one, the unconscious mind will take the path of least resistance – i.e., the more pleasant scenario. However, like most things to do with the mind you can unlearn these techniques and with practice, become the old you! But tell me, for what purpose would you want to?!

4. **Is it best to do a technique just before you ride or the night before?**

   Both are highly effective. You may wish to consider when your trigger point is. Is it the night before or just as you arrive at the stable or just as you get on or only when you start to warm up? Erase the negative thinking before your usual trigger point.

5. **How often should I practise the techniques?**

   It's rather like learning a musical instrument. The more you do your scales, the quicker you can play the pieces.

6. **If I want to compete a month from now, when should I start to do these techniques?**

   ASAP! Give yourself time to practise the ride at home, feeling very safe and secure. If you feel good at home and it's only when competing that your nerves appear, then why not do a practice run and just take your horse to the venue and the collecting ring?

7. **Would hypnotherapy work too?**

   Absolutely! I have had great success with personalised hypnosis for riders. I create individualised scripts for each rider, their horse, their personal goals. This type of hypnosis resonates with the unconscious mind, there's a feeling of familiarity with the scenarios and words that enable to suggestions to be planted deep within the mind.

8. **Which is best, NLP or hypnotherapy?**

   It's horses for courses! Both engage the unconscious mind; NLP uses confusion, visualisation and specific language to enable your mind to change. There is usually something for your conscious mind to be occupied with, so that we can communicate uninterrupted with the unconscious mind. Hypnotherapy uses the same techniques and offers your conscious mind something to do too – concentrating on breathing or relaxing, whilst suggestions are implanted.

9. **Some of these techniques work better for me than others, is that normal?**

   Absolutely! Again, it's what works for you that is going to be the difference that makes the difference.

10. **My friend doesn't really think this stuff works, but she's really nervous. How can I get her to practise these techniques?**

    You can't. You can lead a horse to water……..the only thing that may help a shift in mindset is to see the effect the techniques have on you!

11. **What if these techniques don't work for me?**

    These techniques work if you practise them, have faith in your own ability to change, remove any secondary gain and remember to be at cause. You can always contact me for more information or a free no obligation chat.

12. **Now that I feel more confident, can these techniques help me to improve my performance?**

    Yes! You can use how you are now as a rider as your 'old picture' versus the future you as your 'new picture'.

13. I think it might be better if someone read me the instructions, what do you think?

>That can be fun, but remember, they may not be a certified Practitioner. It's also useful to record the instructions and play them back to yourself.

14. Can these techniques be used outside of equestrianism?

>Yes! I have lots of clients who have seen their worth in other sports and even in the workplace. I have many clients come to me as riding clients, yet we uncover non-riding issues that I also help them to dissolve.

Closing comments

When I was a little girl, we didn't have horses. I loved all things horsey and would look forward to my pony magazine each month, getting my equine fix by quickly devouring the pages. I had lessons at a local riding school and would be happiest just to be there, not necessarily riding, but being with the ponies and horses. When I was about 10 years old, I had to give up riding and it wasn't until I was in my early 30s that I returned to lessons. I was 35 when I had my first horse on loan. Whenever I felt nervous or heard anyone at a competition asking, "Why are we doing this to ourselves?" I'd think of the 10 year old girl who loved horses and how she would have given anything to be at that competition……to be with horses……to have her own horse…..and how I needed to ride like she would have done – carefree and like it was her last ride for 20 years.

R,R &R Chapter 9

Stories are excellent portals into the unconscious mind. Do they have to be true? Absolutely not just plausible! How did that story make you feel?

Everyone loves a good story and I'd love to hear yours - email me at info@traceycolenlp.com

What did you learn? How will you use this to boost your riding confidence?

About the author

Dr. Tracey Cole is a former research scientist, university lecturer and teacher. She now works as a Trainer and Master Coach of NLP, NLP Coaching, Create your Future® and Hypnosis. She coaches and trains clients from all walks of life, including a specialism in helping equestrians train their minds for greater confidence and performance enhancement. Her clients are from around the globe and include professional and recreational riders of all levels and disciplines.

Tracey works one to one in private sessions, as well as leading workshops and seminars and providing high quality board-accredited trainings for personal, professional and sporting development. She does her own mindwork whilst riding and looking after her two mares. She can be contacted at info@traceyclenlp.com or via the website, www.traceycolenlp.com.

You can follow her on Facebook and Twitter

traceycolenlp   @traceycolenlp

Printed in Poland
by Amazon Fulfillment
Poland Sp. z o.o., Wrocław